HOT RELATIONSHIP TOPICS

Secrets of an
Extraordinary Relationship

Melissa Smith Baker

HOT RELATIONSHIP TOPICS
SECRETS OF AN EXTRAORDINARY RELATIONSHIP
Copyright © 2015 by Melissa Smith Baker

ISBN: 9781939812988

Cathy Thorne holds the copyright for the cover cartoon.
Visit her website at everydaypeoplecartoons.com

ACKNOWLEDGMENTS

Above all, I want to thank my husband, Christopher Baker. I wouldn't have an extraordinary relationship to write about if it weren't for him.

And, I wouldn't have written this book if it weren't for Theresa Dintino, my forever-faithful writing buddy, who has critiqued my writing week after week for years.

Special thanks go to the following people for helping me put this book together: Cris Wanzer, my out-of-this-world editor and book designer; Therese Mughannam-Walrath, my longtime friend who catches errors that no one else does; Emily and Edward Winfield, my close friends who support my work wholeheartedly; and Annie Dintino and Mia Szarvas, two young friends who candidly share with me their ideas about relationships from the younger generation's perspective.

I also would like to thank Mary Ellen Baker, my creative web developer, without whom I'd have no presence on the Internet.

Thank you everyone for your encouragement and love.

DEDICATION

To Chris, the love of my life

CONTENTS

ॐ

INTRODUCTION

What constitutes an extraordinary relationship? Are you wondering what it looks like and whether it's possible for you?

When my husband and I almost got divorced in 2002, we had the profound realization that we were humans swimming around in a sea of anxiety. Even after the high-stress time of a near divorce, we were still swimming in anxiety; it just had been reduced to a level that was less painful and more tolerable. We recognized unequivocally that anxiety was forever present; an integral part of the human condition.

For over a decade my husband and I have continued to examine ourselves in our relationship using this lens of anxiety. When we're having a bad time together, we try to recognize and name the anxiety. Sometimes we can pull ourselves back before we reach our maximum anxiety tolerance levels. Where possible, explosions and/or implosions are avoided.

We try not to reach an anxiety level beyond what we can deal with, otherwise we'll blame and shame each other and defend ourselves. Sometimes we succeed and sometimes we don't, but over the years we have gotten better at handling ourselves during high-stress times.

That's what an extraordinary relationship looks like — striving for equanimity in a sea of anxiety and finding that calm place where you and your partner can love each other to the fullest.

To help you and your partner love each other more, I've created a list of twenty-six questions on hot relationship topics such as sex, trust, power, and control for the two of you to contemplate and answer. Don't be surprised if some, or maybe all, of your answers are different from your partner's.

What will you do about the anxiety that arises because the two of you don't agree? Will you react ballistically, withdraw, or respond with equanimity? Since you can't love when you're in a highly anxious state, **how you deal with your fear and anxiety is the secret pathway to love.**

Learning how to love more and fear less is **THE** relationship secret.

To answer these twenty-six emotionally charged questions, you might need some help. Read the following section to find out how to use three simple and effective relationship tools — a special kind of writing, a special kind of hugging, and a special kind of looking.

RELATIONSHIP TOOLS

Quick-Writes
An Easy Way to Access Who You Are

One of the most powerful exercises I introduce to my students is *quick-writes*. If you are asking questions about your relationship, this is a fast and effective exercise that will help you find the answers you are looking for. It's the most potent, self-reflective tool you have at your disposal at any time, any place. (By the way, if you don't want to write, you could draw or paint, following the same rules of the quick-writes.)

What Are Quick-Writes?

These mini, stream-of-consciousness writings are profound. Take any question or sentence completion that you're interested in and write nonstop about it for a couple of minutes, but not more than five. Set a timer. Two minutes can do the trick.

For example, when my husband is driving me crazy and I don't know why, a quick-write helps me check in with myself. The question WHY always begs to be answered. I might start the quick-write by writing the question on the top of a piece of paper or on my computer: *Why is*

Chris driving me crazy? I also could write: *Chris is driving me crazy because...*

Don't censor what you are writing. Some of what you write might be weird or off topic. Just keep going, writing down whatever comes to mind. Don't edit. Don't scratch out. Don't worry about your penmanship or spelling mistakes. Don't take your pen off the paper or stop typing at your computer. This flow will be revelatory to you, one way or another.

When you can't think of something, just keep writing the question or sentence completion. If you have to write the same line a dozen or more times before an idea comes to you, that's fine. You're on track, tapping into your subconscious by writing more quickly than your conscious mind can process.

Reading your quick-writes out loud to yourself afterwards can be an additional way to access your inner self. You can review your writing right away or wait until the next day. You don't have to share what you have written with your partner, unless you want to.

Quick-writes have nothing to do with whether you identify with being a good or bad writer. Writing fast creates a flow that helps access the creative problem-solving imagination of your brain. Discovering your own inner treasure trove will provide you with your own answers.

This method of writing is quite different from journal writing or keeping a diary because it's not self-conscious. Quick-writes can help you every time you feel stuck, stagnant, confused, or upset. Within minutes you'll be thinking about a topic that you'd been ruminating about in a completely different way.

Quick-writes are simple and short, but you'll be amazed by the wealth of personal information that unfolds from them. Do them on a regular basis and your life and relationship will change for the better. Guaranteed!

A Stress-Reliever Hug

Research shows that hugs are healing. There used to be a bus driver in New York City who would hug his passengers when they got on the bus. People would line up for blocks and wait to get their daily hug. There's power in an embrace. You've probably heard about the movement of international huggers who are going around the world spontaneously spreading hug therapy. How can hug energy be infused into a long-term relationship?

Sensual hugging is often part of the sexual repertoire, but how about hugging as a stress reliever? The challenge is learning how to hug your partner in a completely different way; a way that you've probably never thought of.

How To Do A Stress-Reliever Hug

Set a timer for five minutes. Stand comfortably facing your partner. Reach out your arms to lightly embrace each other, but don't lean on one another. It's important that each one of you stands on your own two feet. If your partner is substantially taller than you are, stand on something to equalize the height differential. Don't look at or talk to each other.

Expect nothing from your partner. Concentrate on yourself, on what is going on inside you. You aren't trying to give to or receive from your partner. What you're trying to do is listen to and manage any thoughts or emotions that rise from within you. If you feel physically uncomfortable, shift your weight and try another position. Keep hugging until the timer goes off.

After a stress-reliever hug, if you and your partner want to talk about the feelings and thoughts that came up, it can be helpful, but it's not mandatory. Do the hug at a mutually agreed-upon time on a regular basis.

Why is This Hug Effective?

This kind of special hug symbolizes what you and your partner want to achieve in a healthy relationship, namely to connect with yourself while simultaneously connecting with each other. This simple, transformative gesture has the capacity to put a relationship into a relaxed state. Only then can you and your partner be resourceful enough to love each other.

Dr. David Schnarch, author of *Passionate Marriage*, is a huge proponent of this kind of hugging. He invented it for his clients in his therapy practice. You can read more about it in his book. Give it a try. You have nothing to lose and everything to gain.

When you're bouncing off the walls with excitement, or your children are pushing you over the edge, or if you've just had a marital disagreement, when it's especially hard to reach out and embrace your partner, give yourself and your partner the gift of a stress-reliever hug.

Looking Into
Your Partner's Eyes

It's important to know how to make emotional contact with your partner, both in good times and bad.

Looking at each other is a powerful yet simple exercise that you and your partner can do both in and out of the bedroom.

Exercise

Look into your partner's eyes in a mutually agreed-upon, quiet space. Don't talk. This is not about staring, but about really looking at someone you love and letting yourself be seen. Take the necessary time to get comfortable. Soften your eyes. Relax your face. Make yourself receptive. Let your eyes reach out to your partner from your resourceful, creative, and loving self. Remind yourself of what is wonderful about you and about your partner. Relate to yourself and to your partner, knowing that you and he or she have the capacity to change. You might run into your own resistances, fears, and barriers. Note them in the back of your mind.

Do this exercise for at least five minutes. Setting a timer

can be helpful so that you and your partner don't argue over which one of you ends the exercise first. If you wish, after the exercise discuss with your partner what you experienced, but this is not necessary.

You can do the above exercise either sitting face to face or lying in bed, each one of you with your head on a separate pillow at a distance that works for both of you. It's important to be physically comfortable. Repeat on a regular basis.

Do the above exercise with your partner today. Don't wait to feel great about each other. There's no perfect time. All you have to do is agree to do it and keep doing it until you get the results that you want.

Ironically, it's when my husband and I are *not* getting along that we do this exercise the most. When we're going through a tough time, each day we feel a little change after doing eye gazing. But it might take a week or more before we breakthrough and reconnect. We set the timer and don't talk afterwards because sometimes a few minutes of being with each other is all we can possibly tolerate. The only agreement that we make is to do the exercise — nothing more and nothing less. The energy between us always shifts, and that change of state is what we're looking for.

This special way of looking at each other strengthens

your connection with your partner when times are smooth, and reconnects the two of you when times are rocky.

If both of you open your eyes and look at each other while you have an orgasm, it makes your sexual experience even more intense and moving. It's not that easy to do at first, but keep trying because this deeply personal connection will enhance your relationship.

You'll be astounded to realize that you don't regularly make meaningful eye contact that often with your partner, even if you hang out a lot together. Making the time to look into your partner's eyes can't help but change your relationship for the better.

When answering the following twenty-six questions on hot relationship topics, use these three relationship tools whenever you and your partner get stuck.

HOT RELATIONSHIP
TOPICS

GRATITUDE

Are you grateful to your partner for your relationship?

How often do you say a heartfelt, sincere, not just a perfunctory thank you to anyone, especially to your partner? Probably not often enough.

What does *thank you* mean? It means *I recognize you, I appreciate you, I acknowledge you. I'm grateful for you.*

In recent years, thank yous have gone out of fashion. We're no longer surprised if we don't get a thank-you note for a wedding gift or a thank-you email for a dinner party that we host. It's more likely that we'll be thanked by friends over the age of fifty, but that's not a given anymore.

Why is this trend becoming more and more culturally acceptable? Perhaps with the advent of a freer society without the social etiquette dictates of a more restricted one, the traditional dos and don'ts seem meaningless.

I posit that there's also an underlying psychological component that has contributed to this trend. What many people haven't integrated into their psyche is the paradigm shift of the Copernican Revolution of 1548.

They still believe that being a human living on Earth means they are the center of the universe, that everything revolves around them.

If you believe in this pre-Copernican model, it's fatal for your relationship. The world owes you nothing, and your partner doesn't either. Each and every day your partner makes the **choice** to be kind, generous, and respectful to you, and you do the same vis-à-vis your partner.

Say thank you to your partner without any expectation that he or she will say thank you in return. Relationships aren't quid pro quo — you do this for me and I'll do that for you.

One of my students said that she was eternally grateful to her partner for tolerating her eccentricities, moods, and idiosyncrasies, and that's challenging. No one is easy to live with, and that includes you.

Exercise

Before you go to bed, write down five things that you are thankful for in your relationship. List the small and big ways. Be thankful for what your partner does or doesn't do and for who he or she is. Do this every night for a week. You might keep listing the same things and characteristics night after night, or you might create an ever-growing list. It doesn't matter.

What does matter is getting into the practice of remembering day after day the positive instead of the negative about your partner. It'll help you get a good night's rest and start off the next day on the right side of the bed. Share with your partner what you've been writing and contemplating.

Nowadays there's a plethora of books written on the practice of being grateful when all people need to be reminded of is its power. Gratitude is simple yet life-changing. And, it boils down to two potent words — *thank you* — perhaps among the first words you learned as a child, easy words that can never be overused. A thank-you message *is* the most powerful one you can send to your partner each and every day.

POWER

What's the power balance in your relationship?

Martin Luther King, Jr. said, "Power without love is reckless and abusive and love without power is sentimental and anemic." The ideal is empowered love — love infused with power and power infused with love. How can you enjoy the synergy of these two forces in your relationship?

Partners are always afraid that if they succumb to love, they'll lose their personal power — their ability to direct and shape their own lives, their autonomy. They don't want to live someone else's life; they want to live their own. How do partners integrate power and love instead of giving one up for the other? The answer to this question is *partner equality*.

Example

Let's look at something banal. How about household chores? Who cleans the bathrooms? Even if you're always the one cleaning the toilets, your partner might be cleaning out the kitty litter box. You both know that you have nitty-gritty duties that need to be taken care of and you're willing to divide up these tasks. If you and your partner have a strong sense of who you are and what you're worth, what you're willing to do for the well-being of your relationship, you won't try to coerce or manipulate each other. You'll both know that "cleaning up poop" is part of life.

How do you and your partner handle chores or any other mundanities of life? It might be that you do all the cooking and cleaning and your partner takes care of all the finances and home repairs. This arrangement can work as long as you think it's equitable and fair.

In addition to household equality, understanding what it is to be equal in the psychological realm is vital. This means that you have the power to define what you want, what you think, what you feel, what you believe, and what you do — all of which may be quite different from what your partner wants, thinks, feels, believes, and does. You and your partner are different from each other, yet equal.

No matter how different two partners are externally, the internal psychology of long-lived couples fits together like a puzzle. You resonate with your partner in profound ways that make both of you psychologically compatible. For example, if you suffer from low self-esteem, your partner probably does too. You might manifest your level of self-esteem in the world in very different ways, but you both understand deep down what it's like to not feel worthy.

Equality is about respecting your humanness and the humanness of your partner, as well as what it takes to run a household equitably and to understand yourselves psychologically. Do you see yourself and your partner as worthy of being with each other and of having made the free-will choice to stay together? Healthy relationships are not indentured servitude.

Power imbalances happen when you can't risk the relationship that you're in. This might translate to you being subservient in order to make the relationship happen. The reality is that no matter what you do, your relationship is always at risk because every relationship comes to an end either by choice or death. Your relationship cannot last forever just because you've decided to sacrifice yourself for it. Paradoxically, if you think that you couldn't survive without your relationship, you actually have no power to be yourself within it.

Martin Luther King, Jr. knew that in a society the only way to personal happiness and fulfillment is through equal rights. Love is yearning for power and power is yearning for love. Power and love become degenerative when they stand alone. But when these two forces meld and coexist, their interaction creates equality.

A healthy relationship is the integration and balance of power/love between two individuals who know that they are of equal value, neither one a slave to the other, not to anyone, not to anything.

How does the power/love balance play out in your relationship? Are you straightforward about letting your partner know who you are and what you want?

&

TECHNOLOGY

How does technology impact your relationship?

The average American interacts with some kind of electronic device during his or her free time seven hours per day. Ask yourself the following question: How is technology controlling how you spend time with your partner?

Technology has indubitably changed how humans interact. In my classes, people, young and old, talk about feeling isolated even though they use Facebook and their cell phones to connect to others for many hours per day. Human connectivity and connection are miles apart in how they feel. It's ironic that the more connectivity you have via the Internet, the less connection actually exists. Connectivity can lead to disconnection if you end up spending more time in virtual cyberspace than you do in real physical space with other humans.

The digital world was invented as a tool to enhance your life, not to enslave you. Are you vigilant enough to ensure that the impact is positive rather than negative?

What is preventing you from having a vibrant relationship? Is the culprit technology? If so, are you willing to do something about it? When you and your partner are at the dining table texting your friends, you may be side by side physically, but your play is parallel, not interactive. Don't delude yourself into thinking that it's otherwise.

To make a change, you'll have to dare to be a rebel and go counterculture. You'll have to do something different from your friends and the rest of the world. If you are spending most of your time in virtual reality and seduced by technology more than you are by your partner, do the following assessment of how you spend your time.

Exercises

Take Notes

Write down how you spend your day. Be truthful. What do you do each hour of the day? If you're playing video games, or watching movies or TV shows, are you alone? How much time per day do you actually have a face-to-face conversation with someone, especially your partner? Do you physically touch your partner every day — a hug, a kiss, etc.? After doing this exercise, evaluate and be critical of what you've written. Replace an alone activity with one you can share with your partner. Maybe go dancing or play a board game together. What you do or don't do with your partner definitely determines the quality of your relationship. Once you become conscious of what your day is like, change one activity at a time. You'll soon be choosing satisfying connection over dissatisfying isolation and will be living a more fulfilling life.

Get Unplugged

Here are a couple of ideas to help you and your partner go offline:

1. Agree to go offline at a specific time every evening.

2. Leave your phones in your car while you're having dinner.

3. Instead of emailing your partner, throughout the day write down on pieces of paper ideas and questions that you'd like to share with him or her. Stuff them in your pocket or purse. When you get home from work, share them in person with your partner before you go to bed.

If you and your partner can't agree to do any of the above, start taking breaks from technology on your own and notice whether the quality of your life is better or worse as a result.

One way that technology has helped relationships is the

ease in which you can find getaways on the Net. Thanks to cyberspace, it's easier than ever to find discounted hotels and resorts that can be ideal places to renew and rejuvenate your life together. Go away as often as you can afford to, depending on time and money. And, once you get to your getaway destination, make sure you and your partner agree to spend a large portion of your time together, unplugged.

Since technology connects you to so much information, it usually produces anxiety instead of relaxation. Relationships always work better when partners are relaxed, not stressed.

When my husband and I first got married almost forty years ago, we got rid of our TV set because we were allowing it to interfere in our daily lives too much. We couldn't control that interference unless we got it out of our living space. We wanted to spend time with each other in more creative and participatory ways instead of passively watching hours of shows. When videos were invented, we did get a screen in order to watch what we wanted when we wanted. This is how we controlled our "addiction" to technology. What do you do?

Living in an ever-evolving, high- and higher-tech world can make you feel empowered or disempowered. If you're not in control of how you live your life, someone or something else is. If you think your computer and your cell phone own you, what can you do to own them? For example, can you make the decision to not answer your phone while you're having a conversation with your partner?

Over the last ten years, with the advent of the Internet, I've witnessed something very different creeping into my own relationship with my husband. We parallel play more often, not interacting. Our respective attentions are often elsewhere, not on each other. It's harder to listen to each other because we're so engrossed in what's happening on our separate computer screens.

My husband and I have to continually make more and more concerted efforts to get offline, to stop the Internet invasion from the moment we get up until we go to sleep. It's a screen conspiracy that seduces us away from each other more than we're willing to admit.

Cyberspace is encroaching. Before you know it, it'll gobble up all of your time. If you want a deepening relationship with your partner, you'll have to make some decisions about how you want technology to be part of your life. Think of the ways technology is serving and not serving your relationship. The task of living a balanced life is daunting, but you are the only one who can be vigilant about your choices.

Never forget what Albert Einstein said: "I fear the day that technology will surpass our human interaction." Is technology destroying or nurturing your relationship? Only you can answer this all-important question.

SEXISM

How different are men from women?

When you say, "men are just like that," or "women are just like that," you're stereotyping, not telling the truth. When you make overly generalized pronouncements about your partner, you actually are dismissing him or her. Why would you want to do that? Because you're trying to figure out your relationship dynamics; however, being gender-specific is not the way to understand what's going on. All longstanding single-sex couples have the same relationship issues. In other words, you don't have problems because you and your partner are different genders.

Are men and women so different from each other? Of course, there's the obvious biology. Neuroscience is also discovering that the brains of men and women function differently. They don't even look alike. The structure of the female brain helps women multitask in order to raise children, whereas the structure of the male brain helps men be linear and single-focused in order to procure resources for the family's survival. Despite having non-identical brains, studies show that ultimately the difference between the sexes depends on acculturation and upbringing.

As the roles of men and women morph, the human brain is slowly evolving. You can help the evolutionary process along by not allowing sexism in your relationship. Catch yourself when you start concentrating on your partner's gender. Gender prejudice and bias play a part in your life just as they do in everyone's, just as racism and classism do. But, do you nurture your racist and classist tendencies, or do you try to mitigate them? Racism, classism, and sexism all have something in common: they thrive on dehumanizing and categorizing individuals as "other."

When you get angry with your husband and say, "You're just like all guys..." he can't hear the specifics of what you're trying to tell him because he'll have to defend his maleness. If your husband chides you by saying, "You're acting like all women do..." his deprecating remark is neither constructive nor conciliatory. You won't be able to hear what he has to say because you'll concentrate on justifying your femaleness.

Many long-term couples suffer from these sweeping generalizations about each other's gender. With a counterculture approach, you can begin to put an end to the battle of the sexes in your own relationship. The more you and your partner can remember that you are human beings — not only a man and a woman — the better you'll get along. You both want to love and be loved.

You are both from planet Earth, not from Venus and Mars.

The next time you get together with friends, notice when the conversation turns to male or female bashing. We all have a propensity to do it, and it can even be humorous. Most comedy routines thrive on exploiting these gender stereotypes, and that can be positive. We're not going to be able to hold ourselves back from cathartic laughter. We can, however, defuse gender discrimination by limiting our participation in it and being mindful of where the negative impact edge lies, and not crossing it.

Your partner is an exception to the stereotype you are holding in your mind and heart. Don't discount him or her, or ever lose sight of the individual that your partner is, regardless of gender.

PORNOGRAPHY

What do you think about pornography?

Pornography has come out of the closet. It's no longer wrapped in plain brown paper; it's visible on TV in the living room, and readily available on the Internet. A lot of people worldwide are obviously interested in "pornland." Or, are they just being manipulated by a savvy, multi-billion-dollar entertainment business?

To avoid a debate over semantics, I purposefully define pornography, a loaded topic, very broadly: My definition is *erotica*, whose main purpose is sexual or sensual stimulation and arousal. What's wrong with that? Nothing, unless it leads to violence, misogyny, humiliation, subjugation, denigration, sadism, and/or abuse of yourself or others.

Pornography is not sex education; it's entertainment. Unfortunately, porn is where most people, regardless of age, go to get information about sex. Entertainment is not the same as education. If you are no longer interested in sex, or are pestering your partner every minute for sex, it might be because of your warped expectations influenced by pornography and the media.

Reflect on your own sex education. What and where did

you learn about sexual pleasure, not just about birth control and STDs? Question what you believe your sex life should be like.

There's a lot of misinformation and misunderstanding about sex that contribute to a couple's unhappiness. So, be careful where you are getting your sex education from. How is it aligned with your values and the integrity of the life you've chosen to live?

Pornography is not necessarily toxic, but the industry keeps pushing the envelope in its attempt to normalize all kinds of sexual behavior. Real live partners do not have sex like porn stars, nor do they look like them, with queen-sized breasts and king-sized penises. Healthy partners are not nymphomaniacs who are always eager to participate in extreme sexual practices.

Exercise

I invite you to listen, with or without your partner, to a lively, intelligent, non-moralistic debate about the pros and cons of pornography. Here's a link:

http://www.intelligencesquared.com/events/pornography -is-good-for-us/

The presenters are erudite and articulate. The questions from the audience are thought provoking. It's worthwhile spending ninety minutes listening to this formal debate from England entitled, "Pornography is Good for Us; Without it We Would be a Far More Repressed Society." Afterwards, take the opportunity to think about how this hot topic impacts your own relationship.

Story

A man in one of my classes wanted to forbid his wife from looking at Internet porn. When I asked him whether he thought his sex life, the time they spent together, or her life were being negatively affected by her pastime, he answered no. I suggested that he confront his judgment of how his partner was using her time and think of ways to handle his anxiety that this activity produced for him; namely that it might consume his partner's life and ruin their relationship.

It is indeed frightening that a pornography habit could turn into an addiction that is compulsive, all-consuming, and wreaking havoc in a relationship. Are you or your partner capable of recognizing when your view of sexuality has crossed over into pathology? Into addiction? Are you or your partner fetishizing and objectifying body parts? Are either of you sexually dissatisfied because of not measuring up to pornographic fantasies?

Ultimately, you have to be the one to determine whether you think pornography — soft-core, hard-core, or erotica — is worthwhile listening to, watching, or reading. If you do indulge in this entertainment, be vigilant. Over fifty percent of the couples who get divorced list pornography as one of the reasons they are in court. And, contrary to popular belief, it's not always the guy who is seduced by pornography; thirty percent of the consumers are women.

Men and women destroy their lives because they cannot control their urges and impulses. If pornography is so powerful as to break apart couples, it's obvious that it's worthwhile examining the part it plays in what you believe about sex.

RELATIONSHIPS AS COMMODITIES

Do you know the difference between a fake and a real relationship?

If you have everything — a good job, a nice place to live, good friends, plenty of money — but you don't have a long-term relationship, are you still yearning for one? Are you missing out?

There are lots of factors that contribute to the "no long-term relationship" trend in modern-day society. Here are a few:

- ❖ Technology (Internet, computers, and screens of all sorts) that sucks up many hours per day

- ❖ Easy access to pornography that promotes unrealistic expectations of sex with a real human being

- ❖ Overpopulation, which makes jobs competitive to get and hard to hold on to, which creates stress

- ❖ Female and male rebellion of traditional roles of the stay-at-home mom and bread-winner dad, which turns the status quo upside down

❖ Entitlement of the super-kid generation that is accustomed to immediate gratification

All of the above are some of the reasons why people, especially the younger generation, are unable to hang in there through the thick and thin of a committed relationship.

Many people are also products of non-intact families or of long-suffering parents who define their marriage as a prison sentence. These adults have endured the pain of divorce and/or unhappiness, and they'll be damned if they'll repeat their parents' mistakes. Unfortunately, in their attempt to be empowered, the younger generation in particular may be heading down a slippery slope.

In Japan, in order to have some semblance of human contact, young men and women are resorting to "cuddling" with complete strangers. "Cuddling" is big business; a professional "love" worker can make as much as $800,000 per annum. The curious thing is this: These mafia-run "cuddle hotels" don't include sex.

Obviously, sex isn't what's seductive; it's the contact with another human being. Commoditizing "relationships," however, won't solve the problem of loneliness. What would you prefer? A partner who remembers that romantic trip that you took together twenty years ago, or a stranger, a professional actor, who doesn't even know your name?

Are you settling for anything less than the real thing? Are you willing to take the risk and put the time into a real, vulnerable relationship and pay the emotional price in order to reap the rewards? Will fake, make-believe connection evolve or devolve human psychology? More importantly, regardless of fads and trends, what do you find more meaningful — a real relationship, a facsimile of one, or none at all?

BEING SINGLE

Can you have a fulfilling life when you're single?

The perennial questions for singles are: "How can I meet Mr. or Ms. Right if I can't even get a date?" And, "If I can meet the partner who is right for me, will I be complete?"

When you're trying to find someone to possibly become your life partner, the best thing you can do is live your life to the fullest.

Exercise

Here are some questions to keep asking yourself:

Do I enjoy my work?

If you don't like your work, can you make it interesting or change jobs? If you don't work for a living, do you go to school, volunteer, create art or music? What do you do to keep yourself engaged and excited about life? What you do in your life is what you'll want to talk about on a date. If you don't do anything, you won't be that interesting.

How do I have fun?

Hobbies, adventures, concerts, plays, creating music, football games...what are you excited about that you could share with your date?

What relationships do I already enjoy?

Even if you don't have a partner, do you have other relationships? Maybe with your relatives, your friends, your children, your colleagues, your neighbors, etc. All of these relationships prepare you for a romantic relationship. Maybe you'll find a date through your relationship with your cousin or a friend of a friend.

How do I take care of my health?

Daily hygiene? Exercise? Nutrition? Mental health? No one else can take care of your health for you, and it takes a lot of time and effort. You are attractive to the "right" kind of someone whom you first meet because you are healthy in body, mind, and spirit. Maybe you'll find a date at the health club where you exercise, or at the market where you shop for groceries. And don't forget about sex in the form of self-pleasuring, aka masturbation. You don't have to get a date to have sex with yourself.

Do I have enough money to live well?

You don't have to be rich, but you do need enough to pay for your rent or mortgage, food, and have some extra money for entertainment and anything else that you'd like to pursue. You want to be able to pay your own way for whatever activities you share on a date. You don't want to rely on someone else to pay for you.

What does my home look like?

No matter what your socio-economic bracket is, you can make your living space beautiful by keeping it clean and tidy and decorating it simply and colorfully. When you do meet someone, wouldn't you like to take your date back to a place that you feel good about?

Create and live a life that you're in love with. Don't put your own personal fulfillment on hold until you meet Mr. or Ms. Right. In fact, you won't be able to sustain a vibrant, long-term relationship if you aren't a full and complete person on your own before and during a relationship. (Don't think that a relationship will make or break you, because you are the one who makes or breaks yourself.)

Whether or not a long-term relationship happens in your lifetime, you'll at least have had a marvelous time doing what you love to do.

BEING MARRIED

What is marriage?

Read this poem:

Married Love
You and I have so much love
that it
burns like a fire
in which we bake a lump of clay
molded into a figure of you
and a figure of me.
Then we take both of them
and break them into pieces
and mix the pieces with water
and mold again a figure of you
and a figure of me.
I am in your clay.
You are in my clay.
In life we share a single quilt.
In death we will share one coffin.

— *Kuan Tao-Sheng (1262 to 1319)*

Close your eyes. Take a moment to reflect.
What are your thoughts and feelings about this ancient
poem? Jot them down on a piece of paper before you
read the next poem.

Now read the above poem rewritten:

Married Love
I have so much love for you.
You have so much love for me
that it
burns like a fire,
in which I bake my lump of clay,
molded into a figure of me
and you bake a lump of clay,
molded into a figure of you.
Then we take both of our figures,
each one of us making our separate figures
more beautiful.
I am I.
You are you.
In life we never share a single quilt.
I have my own and you have yours.
In death we will never share one coffin.
I have my own and you have yours.
Side by side we will be buried,
because the only way to be happy
is to know we are two individuals,
coming together, living in the container of life,
loving ourselves.
Only then can we love each other.

Melissa Smith Baker (born 1952)

What do you think of this new version of the previous poem?

If you think that the depiction in the first poem reflects your own thoughts on love and marriage, happiness will continue to elude you. To demythologize your belief system, you must embrace the concept of loving *detachment*, not *attachment*. Paradoxically, this is true love. (Read the "Oneness Myth" in my book, *How to Save Your Relationship...From Yourself: A Myth-Busting Guide to Successful Love*.)

You might prefer the original poem over the way I rewrote it. The first one is fantasy and the second reality. The problem is, fantasy won't help you build and nurture a long-term relationship. Relationships force you to deal with reality head-on. Relationships are not safe, secure, and cozy like this marriage poem implies; they are intense and often wreak havoc in your life.

So, take your lump of clay into the hottest of relationship ovens where you'll create the best figure of yourself that you can, and your partner will do the same. Two people merging as one is an impossibility; humans are not made of clay. And, even if it were possible, you and your partner don't want to strive for oneness, which robs you of personal freedom and growth. Love the sacred hot space that lies between the two of you in the alchemical marriage kiln.

INFIDELITY

I've touched on this topic in my blogs by describing an affair as a theft, a criminal act.

When you have a surreptitious affair while you're still in a committed monogamous relationship, you have committed a crime against your personal integrity as well as against your partner from whom you've stolen choices.

Most people committing adultery are still having sex and a relationship with their "committed" partner. Why? Because they are not willing to take the risk of being honest, which could possibly result in losing both lovers. Most adulterers, be it a sexual affair or an affair of the heart, don't want to leave their primary relationship.

Even though cheaters' websites, such as Ashley Madison, specialize in setting up anonymous liaisons between married people, the majority of extramarital affairs are with people that the couple both know in the same social circles in their neighborhood, school, work, or community.

In some of my classes, students have described that they just couldn't resist the temptation of getting involved emotionally or sexually outside of their committed relationship, that they wanted to lose themselves in someone else, that they weren't consciously looking for a tryst but the opportunity presented itself. My response is this: Never lose your sense of self to anyone, to anything, and that includes your partner. You always have the power to say *Yes* and to say *No;* you are responsible for your actions at all times.

The modern tendency is to normalize affairs, to say that everyone is having them, so why don't couples and society accept them? The issue at stake here is dishonesty, not morality, which is a disservice to yourself, your community, and your children.

Kids are left holding the bag of trauma when their parents split up. Kids are torn apart by the parent who is cheated on who clings, and the parent who cheats who distances. Children are not developmentally able to understand adult issues, they are traumatized by them. Just because high-tech kids appear to be more sophisticated at an earlier age, don't fool yourself into thinking they are any older than they are.

Among professionals there's disagreement about when or if parents should tell their kids about their affairs. Even as an adult child of an unfaithful parent, do you really want to know about the affairs of your parents? Probably not. Children, no matter the age, don't want the fantasy destroyed of who their parents were or what they could have been, and kids desperately want to hold their parents in high esteem.

There are many different kinds of affairs — long-term mistresses, one-night stands, sleeping with your husband's brother, having sex in your marital bed with someone other than your partner, cyberspace lovers, email trysts, serial lovers, etc. There are many degrees of adultery, some more serious than others.

The question to ask yourself is this: Is it honorable to commit adultery, which by definition includes lying and duplicity? Honor isn't a key component of our culture, at least not to the extent it was in the past; but psychologically, honor still plays a key role in how you think about who you are. You must honor yourself in order to love yourself.

The allure of an affair is that it is clandestine and illicit. If you enjoy sneaking around and living a dual existence, you're not an emotionally mature adult, you're not a fully integrated human being. If you can dissociate parts of yourself, you might need therapy to help bring your dysfunctional, fragmented self into a functional whole. Cheating erodes your personal integrity. Don't kid yourself that it doesn't.

Is cheating ever justified? No! If your relationship is intolerable, then have the courage to leave it before, not after, an affair.

The impulse to have an affair can be a wake-up call. If you feel yourself being attracted to someone other than your partner and you can't control your feelings about him or her, then distance yourself from those attractions and try to deepen the relationship with your committed partner. It's natural to feel attracted to others, but it doesn't mean you have to act on your impulsive desire. In fact, it's very sane and rational to not do so.

If you're the one having an affair or you discover that your partner has been cheating on you, it doesn't necessarily mean the end of your committed relationship. Fifty percent of couples do recover and can become stronger than ever, but it takes time and effort to understand what has happened in your relationship. Couples do make mistakes, and not all mistakes are irreparable.

Long-term relationships aren't easy; they test every cell of who we are as human beings.

BEAUTY

Does physical beauty matter in your relationship?

Does a beautiful partner increase or decrease your odds of having a successful relationship? What makes your partner attractive to you? Is it really his or her physical beauty?

The media tells us that attraction is about being young, thin, in good shape, etc. We think that we have to look a certain way in order to be sexy, and our partner has to look this way, too. But, most of us don't fit the criteria. Since we don't meet the beauty requirements, does that mean we can't have a thriving long-term relationship?

Physical beauty is ephemeral. It can't be your capital in a lasting relationship. If your partner was physically "hot" when you first met at age thirty, you can be sure she or he can't sustain that position at the age of sixty. If you're relying on looks — yours or your partner's — to hold together your relationship, you're playing a losing game.

What makes your partner attractive is not really physical attractiveness at all; it's how he or she responds to life and to YOU. Is he funny? Is she creative? Does he have a special *je ne sais quoi*? Does she have vim and vigor?

These are inner qualities that stand the test of time and don't decline, like physical beauty does.

Do outwardly beautiful people have better relationships? Research indicates that the likelihood you will have a healthy and vibrant relationship is much greater as an average-looking person. Why? One reason is because the person of average looks doesn't depend on the outer self to define the inner self to the same extent as someone who is beautiful. This doesn't mean that beautiful people can't be beautiful inside and out, but it does mean that it's harder for them.

The average-looking woman or man has a greater chance of strengthening his or her sense of self. And, that deeper self can cope with the vicissitudes of life and face the challenges of aging with more grace. If your outer looks determine who you are as a person, you are doomed if you live long enough to grow old.

It's actually an advantage having average looks because a long-term relationship can't thrive unless you are capable of cultivating and growing a sense of self. Your average looks help, not hinder, you in attaining that goal.

Stop spending so much time preening and primping. It's what's underneath your exterior that counts the most. You've heard the age-old adage "beauty is only skin deep" a million times, but do you really believe its truth?

It's vital that you do.

Rejoice that physical beauty isn't the key to relationship happiness!

Reflect on how your below-average, average, above, or way-above-average looks have played out in your relationship.

ORGANIZATION

Do you have good organizational skills?

If you have a disorganized, cluttered mind, you'll probably find excuses for why everything else is more important than your partner. You might not want to have sex, have fun, or do anything with your partner until you get everything done that you're thinking about. The problem is, you'll never arrive at that goal because it's not possible. Lists are never-ending, ever-growing. As soon as you get something done, something else needs to be done, and so it goes on ad infinitum.

You can't be clear-headed or creative if what you have to do is spinning around in your mind. So, dumping your to-do lists into a reliable system will help you relax and create time to have more fun with your partner.

Whatever organizational system you use, the top priority is keeping it easy to implement, otherwise you won't do it. Until my husband and I found a system that really worked, we had no idea that organization was one of the keys to a vibrant relationship.

Here are some ideas gleaned from *Getting Things Done, The Art of Stress-Free Productivity* by David Allen. He has the simplest, most effective system ever invented.

❖ If a task takes two minutes or less, stop procrastinating by doing it now. You'll be surprised that most of what you write on your to-do list only takes two minutes or less.

❖ Get your own personal file cabinet. Get a label printer so that your file headings are legible. You can go mostly digital, but there will still be paper that needs to be filed. Make categories for everything, even if a single folder only has one piece of paper in it. Gather up all your papers and notes and create one integrated file system for your work and personal life. Everything in your life that is important and worthwhile should get filed.

❖ Break down an action into parts. People usually don't know what the next action step is. They become overwhelmed if they don't understand all the necessary incremental steps that need to take place to complete a task. For example, if you want to buy your partner a gift, what do you have to do? First, decide what kind of gift you want to give. Then research the gift either on the Net or by going to brick-and-mortar stores. You also have to determine how much you want to spend, purchase the gift, and make a decision about how you want to give it to him or her. (Are you going to wrap it or not? Hide it and surprise your partner?) You'll have to accomplish all of these actions before your partner can receive that gift. Always figure out what your next action step is and you won't find buying gifts such an arduous task, and your partner will appreciate more gifts instead of fewer.

Don't eliminate your romantic relationship from your to-do list. Integrate it into your entire-life file system so that it's never an afterthought. Print your partner's name on a folder and fill it with notes on what to talk about, do, and places to eat and explore together. An effective organization system supports your relationship by making sure that buying a gift for your partner is just as important as giving a presentation at work. A good system will remind you that you don't have to choose your partner over your work or vice versa; that you don't have to forsake one for the other.

Getting organized has had a huge impact on my relationship with my husband. It's only recently that my husband is keeping track of everything, from lists of errands to social dates. And, I now have a file cabinet of my own where I can locate everything at a moment's notice. (Previously, my husband and I shared one.) I no longer feel frustrated that my husband doesn't remember our social calendar, and my husband no longer gets upset that my paperwork is strewn all over the floor. Disorganization is no longer a breeding ground for our stress and conflict.

If you suspect that too little organization is negatively impacting your relationship, do something about it, even if your partner resists. You'll see results, guaranteed. Who would have guessed that getting just the right balance of order in your business and personal life could actually improve your relationship!

ILLNESS

What will you do when your partner has a prolonged illness?

When your partner is seriously ill, you'll need all the help you can get, even though you might not be aware that you do. How can you tie up all the loose ends when your daily life is in upheaval? The best way is to set up multiple circles of support for you, for your partner, and for your family.

When dealing with a long-term, possibly life-threatening illness, get plenty of help, even if you think you don't need it. When your ill partner has to conserve all of her or his energy for healing, you'll need to take care of yourself, and you won't be able to if you and the people who are helping are burning out.

Organize the following three circles:

Form a very large circle. Send out a mass communication to as many friends and family members as possible, near and far. Ask people to sign up for the duty/duties of their choice. The categories may include cooking, driving to appointments or treatments, coming over for visits, food shopping, errand running, researching about a disease, cleaning the house, gardening, checking in on children, caring for pets, fundraising (if you don't have the funds for medical care), coordinating the delivery of meals, etc.

Form a middle-sized circle of twelve people whom your partner personally chooses. Meet on a weekly basis at your home, just in case your mate feels well enough to join in. The purpose of this circle is to fill in all the gaps that the larger group didn't sign up for.

Form a small circle comprised of six people, all of whom your partner handpicks. You may have to help your partner if he or she is too weak to participate. This intimate group is designed to help in the event of death, or the threat of death.

Some friends will be in all three of these circles, some just in one.

For the outer circle, get help from as many people as possible, but choose your two inner, closer circles wisely. Make sure that they are friends and family members who mean the most to you, who can help you and you don't have to help them, and won't upset you or push your buttons or your partner's. Make these two smaller circles work for you and your partner, even though some people may be offended that they aren't the chosen, special members of these groups.

Make sure that each circle has rotating "captains" and the point person is never you. You'll already be overwhelmed.

When facing a major health challenge, these three concentric circles will keep you and your family intact and functioning. Sometimes you'll be disappointed. But most of the time people come through in surprising and magical ways during times of crisis.

෨

PLAYFUL SEX

Is sex with your partner playful?

Being playful sexually seems to be the hardest for partners who have been lovers for a long time. But play and laughter are the glue that sticks couples together — not seriousness. If you're not having sexual fun with your partner, do something right now to turn that around.

Sex is a misunderstood and taboo topic, even in our overly sexualized and liberated society. Often I am told that I can't include the word "sex" in my course descriptions where I teach, even in California! Most therapists, unless they are trained as sex specialists, don't deal with the topic of sex in couples' counseling.

Talking about sex, unless it's in base and crude ways, is off limits in the majority of conversations. People mostly joke about sex. In comedy routines, sexual innuendos abound. People can make fun of it, but can they create their own fun and fulfilling sex life?

Are you having a playful sex life with your partner? If not, here are some suggestions:

1. **Fantasy:** You play out something in your

imaginative mind, either on your own or with your partner. You go into a trancelike, dreamlike state.

2. **Partner engagement:** You talk. You and your partner look into each other's eyes and maybe have eyes-wide-open, eye-to-eye orgasms.

3. **Role playing:** You and/or your partner pretend that you are gods and goddesses, movie stars, superheroes, or whatever else turns you on. You dress up in costumes and/or make up scenarios or scripts.

Integrate all of the above and create an out-of-this-world sexual time. No one way — trance, partner engagement, or role playing — is better than the other, but most of us tend to get stuck in one or two modalities and don't vary our sexual repertoire.

The longer you're with your partner, the more you have to be creative in the bedroom. That might mean digging into your dress-up closet and putting on thigh-highs, your boa, stilettos, or Tarzan costume!

Exercise

Play a hide-and-seek game with your partner, but don't tell your partner that's what you're doing. Keep it a surprise. Here's what to do: Blindfold your partner in the bathroom with the lights on. Tell him or her to not remove the blindfold and not to come out of the bathroom until he or she has slowly counted to 100. That should give you enough time to put the directions on the bathroom floor, close the door, get naked, turn off all the lights in your house, and get yourself to your hiding spot. On the note you've left for your partner, it might read something like this: *Get naked, turn off the light in the bathroom, and come and get me anywhere inside the house. No fair turning on any lights.* What you do after the game is over is up to you!

The older we get, the more the weight of our circumstances and the world dampen our spirits, but that load can be lightened by some sexual fun. Fun is healing. Fun is essential to fulfillment. Fun is not superfluous; it's worthwhile cultivating it. Shared foolishness and laughter actually deepen bonds in a relationship.

GREAT SEX IN RELATIONSHIP

Is it possible to have great sex in a long-term relationship?

The million-dollar question is: Can you have fantastic sex in a long-term, committed relationship? With the predictability of a partner you've known for years, can there still be surprise? Is it possible to reconcile your longing for reliability with adventure in a monogamous relationship? Yes! Yes! Yes!

Sex toys and lingerie are not enough to spice up your sex life. Changing your understanding about the coexistence of sex and relationship will. Sex and an intimate relationship are not an oxymoron. They are not mutually exclusive even though therapists and the media often tell us so.

Unfortunately, couples' therapy is usually divided in two — relationship and sex therapy. Most therapists specialize in one area or the other. This division fosters an unholistic view of a romantic relationship as unintegrated, fragmented, and disassociated. Isn't sexuality part of every couple's life, except for the few who have chosen to be celibate?

The media perpetuates the myth that juicy sex can only be part of the initial stages of falling in love and illicit affairs. Don't fall for what you're reading on the Internet and in magazines. You don't have to do what they tell you to do, which is choose either great sex and not a great relationship OR a great relationship and not great sex. You can have both, but you'll have to take action to wrap up that combo package of sex in a relationship.

Handle Your Anxiety

A long-term relationship invites you to cultivate anticipation, creativity, imagination, playfulness, and novelty. How do you do that? You have to dare to try, and you won't take the risk if you can't manage your anxieties. You won't explore and research ways to have better sex and more sexual fun unless you confront your fears of rejection, failure, shame, and humiliation. People who are only after sex outside of a relationship can avoid experiencing these painful and powerful emotions, but that superficiality stunts their personal growth.

Planning

It's true that duty and responsibility can stifle desire. Long-term couples know that an erotic life often necessitates sex that doesn't happen spontaneously; it has to be planned after the kids are asleep or at a getaway weekend retreat. It's essential to dedicate time to sexual privacy and adventure. Do you and your partner have regular sex dates? If not, why?

If you continue to separate sex and relationship, desire and love, wanting and having, you might enjoy a relationship but miss out on sex. Or, you might explore sex but miss out on a relationship. When you meld the two together and no longer believe in the made-up duality of sex over relationship or vice versa, a long-term relationship is where you can have the best sex of your life. It might not happen every time you have sex with your partner, but the media would lead you to believe that it never does. Don't settle for a relationship that isn't integrated and whole.

BEING OUTDOORS

Do you and your partner enjoy outdoor activities together?

One of the most important things you can do to keep your relationship on track is some kind of physical activity with your partner. What do you do together in the great outdoors — canoe, kayak, garden, jog, hike, etc.?

Walking is the exercise of choice for my husband and me. It's simple and amazingly therapeutic. Over the forty years that my husband and I have been a couple, we've taken thousands of walks together, some more vigorous and others more lackadaisical. The walk doesn't have to be long. Around the block can do the trick. You just have to cultivate the habit of stepping outside and moving one foot in front of the other.

Walking doesn't cost any money. Everybody is capable of doing it, one way or another. It gets you outside in nature (there is sun and sky, even in the city), and away from the sedentary lifestyle that so many people are living these days.

Maybe you're thinking, *Hey, I don't like walking*, or *I can't walk*. Then my rejoinder would be, "Walk any way you can. Maybe that means you go out for a stroll in your wheelchair with your partner pushing you."

On our daily walks, my husband and I usually don't hold hands. My husband always steps a little ahead of me because he's tall and I'm short. It doesn't matter as long as we don't have to shout at each other to be heard. Walking gives us time to be together physically, to talk or not talk.

My husband and I even take walks when we're arguing. We took multiple walks a day when we were on the verge of divorce. It helped us work through our issues and get some exercise at the same time. It also got us out of the house, away from our hiding places.

Sometimes our walks take us all over the place emotionally.

STORY

Last week when we started out on a walk, we were on the same page about the upcoming vacation plans that we were discussing. By the time we got on the trail five minutes from our house, we were in a full-blown argument. I felt so upset that I was ready to turn around and stomp back home on my own. And my husband concurred that it would be a fine idea to do so! I resisted the temptation to retreat and just kept moving forward, one step at a time.

We kept going back and forth with our differing opinions about our vacation, and somehow everything was ironed out by the time we got back home forty-five minutes later. We moved through the *stuckness* of our disagreement by literally moving forward in time and space. We passed kids and moms along the path. We encountered dogs. We saw some beautiful trees and flowers. The colors, the smells, the smiling children all helped us calm down, even though they didn't have any inkling about what was going on with us.

Being out in nature helped us clear our anxious state so that we could get to a different perspective. If we would have stayed home and had a blow-out like this, we wouldn't have been able to move through it so quickly. The act of walking released tension, which got us to the other side, to a place of equanimity so that we could finalize our vacation plans.

In Spain, it's a tradition for everyone to take a *paseo* every night. It's a perfect activity before getting caught up in TV or surfing on the computer. Even if you end up feeling negative emotions such as upset, frustration, or public embarrassment, keep walking together. Let the air and the sunshine, or the sunset, or the moon and starlight mediate whatever is bothering you and your partner.

Take a walk together as soon as possible. The great outdoors is beckoning, waiting for you and your partner to come outside and walk together, no matter where you live — in the city, in the country, or in-between.

IDEAL PARTNER

Is there a recipe for an ideal mate?

Over the years, I've been surprised by how many singles attend my classes. I keep hearing from men and women, young and old, that they are looking for a person who possesses a list of qualities that must be met.

One thirty-five-year-old told me that she had left a few relationships because her partner at the time wasn't a ten, only an eight (on a scale from one to ten). If you think that you need to have a partner that has everything you want, you'll never find him or her.

In 2008, an article in the *New York Times* reported that a seventy-eight-year-old priest in New York City was giving young people advice about whom NOT to marry. Father Pat Connor gave the following advice:

Never marry someone...

who has no friends, who doesn't handle money prudently, whose life you can run, who is too attached to his or her mother, who doesn't have a sense of humor, who is a silent type and withdraws, who is an addict, whose family has characteristics you don't value, who has a different religion from yours, and who doesn't possess good moral character.

Whew! No one on the planet would ever get married if the above criteria had to be met! This list of requisite qualities might sound intriguing, but it's just not true. Why believe counselors and self-proclaimed relationship experts who have never been in a long-term relationship themselves?

What's true is the following: You aren't automatically happy if you marry the "perfect" person.

(Read the "Soulmate Myth" in my book, *How to Save Your Relationship...From Yourself: A Myth-Busting Guide to Successful Love.*)

Many couples who are "meant" for each other don't know how to navigate the peaks and valleys of a multi-decade relationship. Why not? Because they don't have an understanding of relationship dynamics — how they develop, how they force you to grow up, change, and learn about who you are.

The "ideal" mate is not a prescription for a successful relationship. Divorce courts are filled with couples who thought they'd married the man or woman of their dreams. What guarantees success is your capacity to understand love, intimacy, sex, desire, commitment, stress, and connection — and how these concepts play out in your relationship. This is why relationship education is so important. (Read the chapter "Something

Feels Wrong Myth" in my book, *How to Save Your Relationship...From Yourself: A Myth-Busting Guide to Successful Love.*)

When you read newspapers, magazines, and books, do not pay attention to checklists such as this. Everyone wants a sure bet, but it doesn't exist. If you are clueless about what's happening in your relationship, Father Connor's ideal criteria won't be able to guide you and keep your relationship going through the thick and thin of life. Friends, zero addictions, and fine moral character won't help if you don't understand how relationships function in the real world.

MONEY

What are your money demons?

Conflicts around money are the number-one reason why couples get divorced. While it's impossible to be in agreement with your partner about every aspect concerning your finances, you can prevent money issues from breaking your relationship apart.

Here are four questions you and your partner need to ask yourselves and each other:

What are your childhood memories regarding money?

Did your parents tell you money was bad or good? Did your parents argue about having too little or too much of it? How you deal with money now was formed when you were very young. Access those unconscious ideas and bring them to your consciousness. If you don't deal with these money demons (and everyone, rich or poor, has them) they — not you — will run your financial life.

How do you deal with credit cards and loans?

Are you in debt? The only debts that make sense to take on are for your home, car, health, education, or a business venture. Try to never use your credit card except when you have to, such as for plane tickets, rental cars, and Internet purchases. By being judicious about when to use cards, you'll automatically save thirty percent. Studies show that credit and debit cards don't have the same psychological impact as paying with cash. Plastic isn't real. Greenbacks are. Put the cards away, even if you're seduced by the airline miles that you'll accumulate. Don't be fooled into thinking that they're free.

Who's in control of your finances?

You or your partner? How do you split up the responsibilities of bill paying and investing? Do you alternate your duties? Try to meet at least quarterly with your partner to go over your financials. Discuss what's working and what's not. Money is an emotionally charged topic since it's primal — it's about survival. Most couples won't touch it with a ten-foot pole. So, money remains the elephant in the room. Over fifty percent of couples don't have wills or won't discuss estate planning because they can't bear the upsetting feelings that the topic of money can cause. Even if the meetings with your partner result in arguments, don't avoid them. They will get easier the more often you have them.

How affluent do you want to be?

How are you saving for your retirement? How long do you want to keep working? Do you want to keep accumulating wealth by continuing to work, or would you rather simplify your life, downsize, and retire early? When is enough, enough? There are so many questions that you might need some help from a financial advisor to tease them apart and resolve them.

Money issues are gut-wrenching. Over the four decades of my marriage, my husband and I have had some of our ugliest moments discussing money. Fortunately, confronting money demons is one of the catalysts that also makes relationships healthier and less dysfunctional.

It's a rough road that you and your partner will have to take sooner or later.

Have the courage to walk the money-talk path right now. Start that journey by reading my book, *Le Budget Envelope Game: Get More Cash Flow In Your*

Relationship. It's a simple and fun budget system that my husband and I invented and have been playing for years.

ॐ

MEANING FLEXIBILITY

What meaning do you give to what happens in your relationship?

Humans are meaning makers, meaning machines. We assign meaning to everything. It is the meaning that we give to what happens in our lives that creates the feelings that we have, and consequently the conflicts that arise from those feelings. Meanings are wired into each one of us from our own past experiences, which means that when we change our thinking, we change the meaning we once gave to something in our lives. This flexibility of meaning enhances your relationship with yourself and your partner in myriad positive ways. The more flexible you can become, the happier you will be.

Story

When I see a little bit of chaos and disorder, oddly, it makes me feel happy. It means fun and creativity to me because of the environment in which I grew up — a lively household in disarray. My husband, however, would probably interpret the same scene as a mess and feel negatively about it. A disorganized atmosphere might make him feel uncomfortable because he grew up in an orderly household.

Two different meanings of the same space. Who is right? Neither one of us. And both of us.

After a few decades of living with my husband, my meaning has grown to encompass more possibilities. Now I can have plenty of creative expression in places that are in and out of order. My meaning flexibility has given me more freedom because I can be creative in many different venues — messy and cleaned-up.

Breaking free from programming isn't easy. My feelings about creative chaos are from my parents, who both thrived in cluttered and stuff-out-of-place spaces. Is this the ambience I really need for my creativity?

Having a broader repertoire of responses, instead of just one, makes for a more organic and interesting relationship. Having a partner who sees the world differently helps you realize that any given meaning isn't right or wrong; it's a limited way of interpreting something. (Read "The Reality Myth" in my book *How to Save Your Relationship...From Yourself: A Myth-Busting Guide to Successful Love.*)

At first, you might hesitate to exchange one meaning for another because you may be too attached to what your meaning says about your identity, or you may think you've capitulated to your partner's meaning. You may think it's delusional to be so wishy-washy. This is false thinking because all you are doing is trying on glasses of various prescriptions that make you see your world differently.

Becoming an expert at meaning flexibility minimizes relationship dissatisfaction. Playing with different meanings of your relationship issues might help you resolve them. You'll never be able to hold on to one meaning that will serve you for a lifetime. One meaning might work for a while and then you'll need another to replace it as you grow wiser. For me, the meaning of chaos in my life is going to keep morphing.

Practice conscious meaning flexibility on a regular basis and you'll be happier. Don't hold back from manufacturing countless, different pairs of "meaning" glasses.

❧

CONTROL

Do you discipline your children, but not yourself?

Being a parent puts tremendous stress on the mother and father. If your children are driving you crazy, usually your first reaction is to get them to behave. Perhaps yelling has become a pattern, your coping mechanism, and you'd like to change it because it's not productive. Here's my advice. Instead of trying to control your kids, first control what's going on inside you. It's the only way to build parent/child trust. When your kids witness you handling your emotions, and not flying off into a rage, it makes them feel safe and taken care of.

Remember that your children are stressed out as much as you are. Most kids are overwhelmed by all of their activities, babysitters, and school. You don't have to shout at or discipline (which is another word for control) your children. All you have to do is control yourself. It might seem counterintuitive, but it works. How can you quickly settle yourself down in the middle of any scenario that may arise?

Exercises

Here are two very effective parenting skills:

Breathe

When you can't handle a situation, take deep breaths. Inhale. Exhale. Breathe as slowly as possible. Slowly count your breaths if it helps you calm down. You can do this at any time and in any place. If you can do something as simple as being conscious of your breathing, you'll oxygenate your brain and will be able to think of a resourceful and creative way to manage the chaos. If you hold back for a moment and don't jump into the fray, you'll gain perspective and know what's really going on and how to address it. You'll be able to show your children that there are many ways to respond positively instead of reacting negatively to any given situation. This parent-to-child gift is priceless.

Hug

If you and your partner are together when you feel overwhelmed by your children, try something innovative and unexpected that will catch the kids off-guard. Do a special kind of relaxing hug that is described at the beginning of this book. If your children see their mom and dad hugging, that embrace will automatically calm them down. They might even want to join in the hug with the two of you.

Having a happy home environment is not about disciplining your children, it's about what you show your children as role models. Can you discipline your own emotions, your level of stress...the very thing you're asking your kids to do? When you're balanced and not out of control, your children see that you have respect for yourself and for them, which helps prove that you're ultimately capable of loving them.

TRUTH

Do you tell the truth?

It's a natural, primal, survival instinct to hide. You actually can't be human without hiding something about what you do/did or who you are/were. Hiding is how we humans have survived. However, this hiding-out from ourselves and others leads to secrets and lies and the dysfunction that they create.

Supposedly, humans tell about four lies a day. Here are some ways that you might be lying on a regular basis: Do you chronically say you'll be ready at a designated time and are more often than not late? Do you tell half-truths about how you spend the weekly budget because you don't want to hear your partner's admonishments? Do you make excuses about your unacceptable temper tantrums? Are you an addict — alcohol, sex, drugs, work, etc. — and don't admit that you are?

We all lead soap-operatic lives. Often the secrets are sexual in nature. Perhaps you had a long-term affair with your sister's husband or your brother's wife. Or, maybe you are having a short-term, clandestine affair now or have had one in the past that you never told your partner about.

You might think that your relationship is free and clear of shame, dishonor, deception, and duplicity since these are harsh accusations. You might not be an addict or an adulterer, but aren't you guilty of telling little white lies, or pretending, or not telling the whole truth and nothing but the truth? Every couple deals with transgressions of varying degrees, and every one, big and small, takes its toll on a relationship.

What can you do about your toxic trove of secrets and lies?

Exercise

Write down your secrets and lies, and say what you're willing to do about each of them. Some of them you can do something about right away, while others can wait. (Remember that you don't have to share everything with your partner, all your thoughts and actions. You do have a right to a private life. A private life, however, is different from a secret one.) This doesn't mean that you have to have a truth-telling session, confessing all your "sins" to your partner. It means that you have to tell the truth to yourself. Once you do that, you'll know what to say or not say to your partner. This painful list-making can be a cathartic opportunity to see yourself and your relationship more clearly. Facing your fears will release you from shame. Get professional help to go through this courageous process if you need it.

Story

I try to clean up and detoxify my *relationship house* on a regular basis, but it took me decades to stop doing a particular childish behavior. I'm actually ashamed to admit that I did this for such a long time. This is what I used to do: I used to tell my husband that I would be home at a certain time and then return home much later. I wouldn't call and be considerate enough to inform him of my revised return time. I used to just come back home whenever I wanted to.

Why didn't I tell him that I didn't know when I'd be home and not to worry about me? Was it passive-aggressive or defiant on my part? I didn't have a history of my parents or my husband getting angry with me for returning home later than expected. My husband never made a big deal about it, except to say I should have told him the truth — and he was right.

When I recognized what I was doing, which was wanting to be free without any constraints on my time, I started being honest. I could finally state what I wanted. "I'll be home, but I don't know when. If it's past midnight, I'll give you a call."

How can you clean your *relationship house?* It's going to get dirty again and again. It's normal. Be an adult and start a regular cleaning cycle.

It's important not to beat yourself up, because lying and hiding are part of the human condition. What you're trying to do is be conscious of this less-than-honorable behavior that damages you and your partner. Once you can admit that you're doing something that's not serving your relationship, there's a greater likelihood that you'll be able to do something about it.

Sweeping relationship toxicity under the rug is not possible forever; it eventually surfaces. You can't successfully hide from yourself because life is asking you to be the best and most enlightened being you can be. Do more than survive — THRIVE!

GUILT

Can you admit when you are wrong?

It's hard to be criticized by your partner because you want his or her approval, even if you think you don't. Can you admit when you're wrong?

Story

One evening my husband and I were preparing dinner together. I finished making the salad and dressing. While I was waiting for some fish to cook that my husband was grilling, I checked on emails in the den. When my husband called me for dinner, I finished up what I was working on. Five or ten minutes passed before I arrived at the table. By then my husband was already eating, and was upset that it had taken me so long to come to the table.

At first, as a way of justifying my tardiness, the thoughts in my head went immediately to my husband's inconsiderate table etiquette, of how often he gets up too early and leaves me at the table all alone. While this may be true, it didn't give me the right to not be punctual. My husband's disapproval of me not coming to the table on time was the issue at hand, not something from my husband's past behavior that I was using as a weapon, my defense. (I hate to admit how often I use this juvenile tactic to not accept responsibility for my actions instead of following the Golden Rule!)

Once I realized I was wrong and could see how I was damaging our time together, my husband and I were able to have a conversation about how important it is to eat dinner together. It's been a sacrosanct tradition for us for almost forty years. We reaffirmed that eating dinner together is a meaningful ritual that we wanted to continue.

Think of a time with your partner when you've denied that you were culpable. How could you have lessened the pain by hitting it head-on? Whether this happened last night or ten years ago, if you can talk to your partner about the incident, this could be the opportunity to heal a wound and prevent new ones.

Sometimes we adults act like children. We can't handle being criticized. We think that we even have a right to our reactions. Well, we do, but can we catch ourselves if our reactions are too defensive or extreme, and reframe them? Can we ultimately behave like an emotionally mature adult, admitting that we are wrong, and move forward without the heavy emotional baggage that we usually like to create and carry around?

Lightening up is about accepting ourselves when we're not right. When we do something wrong, it doesn't mean anything about who we are, except that we made a poor choice and that we have the possibility to choose more wisely next time.

SELF-RIGHTEOUSNESS

Are you self-righteous?

What if your partner has a habit that bugs you? When you hear yourself complaining about one of your partner's habits time and time again, stop and ask yourself, "Why does it bother me?"

Did you ever stop and think that maybe you're being self-righteous?

Story

I sometimes get upset when my husband's socks are on the floor and I feel I have to put them in the laundry. As you already know from reading this book, I'm not a neat nut and my husband is the more efficient one, but not when it comes to socks on the floor. Why do dirty socks irritate me? I've already told my husband that this habit bothers me and he keeps doing it anyway. Does it make me feel disrespected? What actions can I take? I could say nothing and keep picking up the socks and get resentful, or be shaming and make my husband do his own laundry.

How can I get this habit to stop pushing my buttons? In the case of my husband's socks, I changed the tapes in my mind. I stopped telling myself that I'm the one that has to pick up after him, that I'm the one who is always being put upon. The truth is he picks up after me, too. He tolerates my piles of paper in the corner of our bedroom, waiting to be filed — the heaps of "important" projects that are probably just as annoying to him as his socks are to me. I stopped being self-righteous, which means that I stopped holding a position of moral superiority over my husband.

When I can laugh and acknowledge that we both have our idiosyncrasies and foibles that are aggravating to each other, there's no need to take our habits personally. When I've gained a different non-self-righteous perspective, I realize it doesn't matter whether I pick up his socks. Sometimes I do and sometimes I don't. I'm free to decide because I've acknowledged that I have a habit that is just as crazy-making for my husband as his socks are for me. My character is not superior to my husband's just because I pick up my own dirty socks and put them in the laundry!

You can be successful at stopping the negative tapes spinning in your mind, but you first have to admit that you, too, are just as annoying to your partner as he or she is to you. But you won't be able to do that if you're self-righteous. You'll have to get off your high horse. Having to be right doesn't indicate that you're confident and that you have a strong sense of who you are; it actually can mean just the opposite — that you're insecure.

Having to be right all the time is an avoidance technique, a cover-up that is dysfunctional. Can you stop thinking that you're always correct and that your partner is mostly wrong? Ask yourself if you have a habit that irritates your partner. If you can't think of one, you're not thinking hard enough. It could be your insufferable self-righteousness.

ARGUMENTS

What do your arguments and triggers mean?

What are emotional triggers that set off arguments? If your partner's behavior or a statement that he or she makes reminds you of something from your past that you haven't resolved, you'll get upset. When you reach a level of internal discomfort that you can no longer tolerate, you'll explode or implode. Why? Because the unresolved emotional pieces are running amok, unmetabolized inside you. This is what manifests that out-of-control moment when you lash out at your partner and go ballistic, or withdraw and/or beat yourself up emotionally.

You can't be human and not have triggers. They explain why you act a certain way, but they do not excuse you from the damage you cause. When you were a child, you unconsciously used coping mechanisms in order to survive. You did the right thing. Fighting or retreating might have been what you had to do. However, as an adult, the challenge is becoming conscious of the triggers and mitigating them.

The Life of a Trigger

The first place you'll find the trigger is in your body, since it automatically makes you feel bad. It takes lots of skill to find the precise trigger for every negative emotion or mood that you're experiencing, but it's possible if you remember the following:

❖ It's not your partner's fault that you are reacting the way that you are. What sets you off has nothing to do with anyone else, only with the emotion that is already inside you.

❖ The only question that you need to ask yourself when you get triggered is: Why am I *reacting* instead of *responding*?

❖ There is no way to control another person's behavior, and that includes your partner's, because every human being is a free agent. Your only choice is to control your reaction.

❖ Your partner is often the catalyst (aka trigger) for you to look at what has been bothering you from a time in your life that predates your partner. Is there something from your past that is being triggered in the present?

❖ You don't have the right to be a "control freak" and

have everything your way in order to feel at ease. You must learn how to cultivate flexibility and resilience. There are options other than fuming and/or yelling. There's always an array of possibilities if you can calm yourself down enough to envision them.

Arguments can be destructive or constructive, unhealthy or healthy. If you understand your trigger, these uncomfortable conversations, discussions, or debates can become a more acceptable part of you and your partner's dynamic. Relationship conflict is completely normal, an integral part of relationships, not something to avoid, fear, and dread.

Arguments, especially those with partners, are actually opportunities in disguise to stop playing the victim, take responsibility for life choices, and emotionally grow up...if and only if you confront your trigger.

NARCISSISM

Are you or your partner a narcissist?

All humans are at least a little bit selfish because we want what we want. How we go about getting what we want puts us on a narcissistic continuum. When it comes to relationships, it's important to know where you sit on the narcissistic spectrum. On a scale from one to ten, are you a little bit selfish or do you have a narcissistic personality disorder? Do you have the chronic narcissistic habit of never being on time? Do you care if you waste other people's time so long as they don't waste yours? If you are constantly busy doing what you want to do and that's all that counts, and never think of others — especially your partner — you might stop to take a look at what number you are on the narcissistic scale.

Narcissism is actually extolled as a virtue in modern-day culture. Our media glorifies getting what you want. The culture supports the narcissistic goal of getting what you want most of the time at all costs, but narcissism wreaks havoc in a relationship.

Story

My husband has been complaining for decades about

my habit of going to bed after midnight. He likes to go to bed earlier than I do, and because he's a lighter sleeper than I am, getting a good night's sleep isn't easy for him. I always wake him up when I finally come to bed, and he can't fall right back to sleep afterwards. I, on the other hand, sleep like a rock.

We'd have our usual perennial arguments about what time to go to bed. I'd change my habit for a while, and then go right back to what worked for me. It wasn't until I was writing this chapter that I realized that I really didn't care about my husband's grievances. I only paid lip service to them. I just wanted to do what I wanted to do — which is to stay up as late as I wanted. When I realized that I had complete disregard for his feelings in order to get what I wanted, I changed my behavior immediately.

I don't want to be a narcissist, even if at times I act like one. Now I'm in bed with my husband at an earlier hour. And, if I want to go to bed later, then I need to sleep on the couch, not with my husband. I don't need to get what I want at the expense of my husband's well-being.

Can you examine your part in your relationship to see if there's any narcissism there that you'd like to eradicate? It's never too late. For my relationship, it's a relief to have resolved our marital bedtime issue.

But what about a more serious relationship issue, such as an extramarital, surreptitious affair? It measures high on the narcissistic scale because an affair is really about stealing your partner's choices without him or her knowing about it. You want to have your cake and eat it, too; have your partner and an extra one on the side. You've become a thief; you've actually committed a relationship crime. Stop your criminal actions and take the risk to come clean, even if it means that you end up losing both lovers. Keeping your personal integrity should always be your top priority. (Read the chapter titled "Infidelity" in this book.)

If you are doing anything to the detriment of your partner, can you stop that narcissistic behavior? I changed my behavior because I didn't want to be a person who didn't care about my husband's feelings just to get what I wanted. If you don't value narcissism as a way of being, you'll have to do something different, too. What could that be?

THERAPY

How important is therapy for a successful relationship?

I often hear about newly engaged couples going to counseling and I cringe at the thought.

Counseling is not what couples need the most; they need education about relationships. Why? Because it normalizes, not pathologizes, relationships.

Have you ever taken a course on long-term relationships? Probably not. Most people haven't. Have you studied your own relationship? What are love, intimacy, sex, desire, stress, commitment, freedom, connection, personal growth, and relationship dynamics? Do you know how to take care of yourself as your relationship unfolds? When you understand these topics, you will know how to have a vibrant and fulfilling relationship.

Most of us are not too screwed up to sustain a long-term relationship once we know what one is. The process of learning and discovering new, transformative information is a fun and exciting exploration.

Unfortunately, our only model for relationship help is a therapeutic one that hasn't been that successful. The divorce rate continues to be high.

Seeing a therapist should be short-term in the majority of cases. The ancient Chinese proverb says it best: "Give someone a fish and it feeds them for a day. Teach someone to fish and they have food for a lifetime." Therapy should not become a crutch, because you need to learn how to become your own therapist. There are times, however, when you'll definitely need professional guidance. My husband and I wouldn't still be together if we hadn't found a therapist to help us through the hardest moments.

When you're seeking help, here are some questions to ask a prospective counselor:

1. What are your views on divorce? (What's your own marriage history?)

2. What kind of therapy do you practice? What is your paradigm? Can you recommend your favorite book or website on relationships?

3. How do you deal with sexual issues during your counseling sessions?

4. How long are most of your clients in therapy?

5. How long have you been practicing and what's your success rate? What's your definition of "success"?

Make sure you interview several therapists. If a therapist has been married multiple times, can't tell you what kind of therapy he or she practices, doesn't deal with sex, sees the same clients for decades, or can't recommend a book to read, don't choose that therapist. Even if you're feeling desperate for help, be picky about your decision because therapy is expensive and often ineffective. In addition, don't think you have to like your therapist. Actually, your therapist shouldn't be your friend, but you do have to respect him or her.

Remember that therapy is not the first place to turn; it's the last resort. Get some relationship education first. Visit my website at lovingforkeeps.com and get started now.

TRANSFORMATION

Do you feel remorse and compassion for yourself and your partner?

Before you die, how will you respond to the only question that matters: "Do you know how to love and to be loved?" You and your partner do and say many hurtful things to each other, but forgiveness isn't the pathway to love and being loved, the transformative power of remorse and compassion is.

In 1970, the hit movie *Love Story*'s only memorable line was, "Love means never having to say you're sorry." This might be truer than you think.

Story

In my own marriage, I've had to examine my passive-aggressive behavior about making my husband wait for me. Until I could feel remorse, which is more than regret, I made no lasting changes in my behavior because "sorry" was just too easy to say and not really mean. Often, I'd say "I'm sorry" just to appease my husband's negative reaction to my lack of punctuality, not because I understood how my behavior was eroding our relationship.

One day I realized that I was doing to my husband what my dad had done to my mom and me — always keeping us waiting for him. Here I was, expressing the same disregard that my father had for time and his loved ones' feelings. In order to change my behavior, this is the process I had to go through: First, I felt the painful responsibility for the lack-of-punctuality arguments that could have been avoided had I only been on time, and had been a woman of integrity. Then I felt guilt and shame for my egregious repeated behavior. It was only after experiencing this excruciating grief that I could finally cultivate compassion for myself and my husband.

Here's the thesaurus.com definition of the difference between regret and remorse: "Regret carries no explicit admission that one is responsible for an incident, while remorse implies a sense of guilty responsibility and a greater feeling of personal pain and anguish." For decades I couldn't admit to what I had been doing until I felt the responsibility of remorse for my actions.

Here's the dictionary.com definition of compassion: "Feeling of deep sympathy and sorrow for another who is stricken by misfortune, accompanied by a strong desire to alleviate the suffering." I was the one who was inflicting the pain because of my lack-of-punctuality habit.

After feeling remorse, self-compassion was the salve that

I applied to my wounds. The healing was complete when I could also feel compassion for my husband, whom I had repeatedly disrespected by making him wait around for me time after time. He was justified in being angry even though I usually insisted that he was over-reacting; that my injurious behavior wasn't a big deal, just a minor infraction. Why couldn't he get over it? It obviously didn't bother me as much as it bothered him because I was the perpetrator.

You can't nurture a relationship by uttering hollow apologies. That's why "love is never having to say you're sorry" is just too superficial. To sustain love, the depths of remorse and compassion must be excavated, understood, and expressed.

Every couple, bar none, participates in behavior that cries out for transformation. The two-pronged path of remorse and compassion is how to get back on the love track of loving yourself and your partner.

Identify one repeated behavior that you're responsible for in your relationship that needs the healing love of remorse and compassion for which a simple "I'm sorry" would not suffice.

CONCLUSION
GETTING UNSTUCK

Recurring conflicts that revolve around hot relationship topics take long-term relationships to narrow, uncomfortable places. It's normal to get stuck in these slot canyons. The steps below will help you climb out and resolve issues.

This simple but profound process works each and every time:

1. When you're in a rough place, your stress level skyrockets. If you can't manage your stress in healthy ways, you can't go on to steps #2 and #3. (For more information, read the "Anxiety and Stress Myth" in my book, *How to Save Your Relationship...From Yourself: A Myth-Busting Guide to Successful Love*.)

2. Once you are calm, you can respond instead of react to whatever comes your way. If you can't deal with the stress, you'll react by being angry or upset. You can only be responsive when you feel calm enough to self-reflect.

3. Self-reflection is what will help you become

creative at brainstorming and capable of making breakthroughs. If you keep hiding or running away from yourself, you won't be able to understand how to get unstuck.

Remember this formula: CRS. **C**alm yourself down, **R**espond instead of react, **S**elf-reflect.

Anytime you feel uncomfortably stuck, first settle yourself down. It's the most important thing you can learn how to do in life. This is why successful couples need to become expert stress-managers.

Wise, creative, and resilient problem solving is never possible in a highly reactive state. A stressful state is not capable of finding answers. Cultivate an inner state of calm, and you'll know how to get out of any relationship slot canyon.

Congratulations!

You have answered twenty-six difficult, thought-provoking questions. You have earned your master's degree in relationship anxiety management. You're now ready to enter the PhD program. You and your partner need to become experts because "Love is the only sane and satisfactory answer to the problem of human existence" (Erich Fromm).

If you have any questions, please contact me at mel@lovingforkeeps.com

Blessings on your relationship journey!

About Melissa Smith Baker

As a couple, my husband and I enjoyed a vibrant social life, romantic getaways, daily walks and talks, parenting, and travel. Despite having so much going for us, we were on the verge of divorce in 2002.

Once on the other side of our crisis, our marriage was not just intact but thriving. I started talking to family and friends about what my husband and I had learned. I witnessed their relationships improving because of the information I was sharing with them. In order to reach more couples and singles, I decided to create a website, blog, give talks, write relationship books, and develop an innovative curriculum called *Loving For Keeps.*

My books *How to Save Your Relationship...From Yourself: A Myth-Busting Guide to Successful Love* and *Hot Relationship Topics: Secrets of an Extraordinary Relationship* are part of my *Loving For Keeps* classes. I also wrote *Le Budget Envelope Game: Get More Cash Flow In Your Relationship,* because a component of my relationship curriculum is about money. Understanding money is key to a successful relationship.

For over a decade I have been a relationship teacher, author, and speaker. I meet my students in all kinds of locations — at retreat and community centers, spas, bars, health clubs, cafés, corporations and nonprofits, private homes, conferences, therapists' offices, and even grocery stores. I also teach virtually anywhere in the world. Everyone, young and old, wants to know how to have a fantastic romantic relationship. Don't you?

Change your life by getting some relationship education. My husband and I didn't break up; we got educated, which means that we now understand our relationship in new ways. After more than forty years together, we're happier than ever.

∾

Find out more about my public and private classes or about how to hire me as a speaker.

Visit my website: lovingforkeeps.com
or
Contact me at mel@lovingforkeeps.com

Other Books by

Melissa Smith Baker

How To
Save Your Relationship
...From Yourself

Cathy Thorne © www.everyday-people-cartoons.com

TO LOVE, HONOR, AND ANNOY.

Myth-Busting Guide To Successful Love

MELISSA SMITH BAKER

Also Available in Spanish!

If you are wondering how to save or enhance your relationship, this book is for you. It is written in short chapters for people who want to get to the core of how to have a successful relationship. Happy, long-term couples exist, but how do they do it?

How to Save Your Relationship...From Yourself takes 31 relationship myths and shakes them up so you can see what is truth and what is fiction. Within ten minutes of reading, you will have tools to start building and sustaining a vibrant and healthy relationship.

LE BUDGET ENVELOPE GAME

GET MORE CASH FLOW
IN YOUR RELATIONSHIP

MELISSA SMITH BAKER

Tired of spending beyond your means? Feeling out of control of your finances? Wishing you could afford your dream vacation? Got stress in your relationship over money? If you answered yes to any of the above questions, then play **LE BUDGET ENVELOPE GAME!**

Try a cash-only budget that uses envelopes to help you save thousands of dollars per year. In only one minute per day, you can save money in a fun and easy way. Simple directions. Forget about time-consuming record keeping. All you need to play is envelopes, paper, and a pen. Anyone can play — singles and couples — if you know how to add and subtract. You don't even have to calculate anything before you start.

Once you start, you'll never stop playing **LE BUDGET ENVELOPE GAME**. It will enhance your sense of empowerment and enrich the quality of your life.

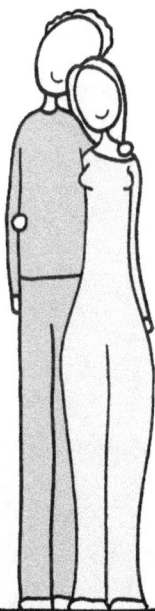

www.ingramcontent.com/pod-product-compliance
Lightning Source LLC
Chambersburg PA
CBHW021130020426
42331CB00005B/702